AMAZING
MIGRATIONS

LAND

Harriet Brundle

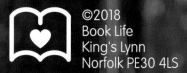

©2018
Book Life
King's Lynn
Norfolk PE30 4LS

ISBN: 978-1-78637-221-5

Written by:
Harriet Brundle

Edited by:
Kirsty Holmes

Designed by:
Gareth Liddington

A catalogue record for this book
is available from the British Library.

Photocredits: Abbreviations: l-left, r-right, b-bottom, t-top, c-centre, m-middle. All images are courtesy of Shutterstock.com.

CoverBg – Jurgen Vogt, CoverTl – Maryna Pleshkun, CoverBl – davidhoffman photography, 2 – Eduard Kyslynskyy. 4 – Delbars. 5t – Juergen Wackenhut. 5b – Markus Gann. 6ml – Jeff McGraw, 6m – davemhuntphotography, 6mr – Patila, 6bg – Paula French. 7m – umpo. 7bl – Xseon. 7br – Rusla Ruseyn. 8 – Sergei Kolesnikov. 9 – Dennis W Donohue. 10l – Tatiana Dorokhova. 10r – conrado. 11 – davemhuntphotography. 12 – GUDKOV ANDREY. 13 – Arturo de Frias. 14 – Jeff McGraw. 15 – longtaildog. 16 – Volodymyr Krasyuk. 17 - Ian Usher. 18 – Patila. 19 – shaftinaction. 20 – kwest. 21 – meunierd. 22l – riff. 22r – Drew Rawcliffe. 23l – Artens. 23r – Matej Ziak.

Images are courtesy of Shutterstock.com. With thanks to Getty Images, Thinkstock Photo and iStockphoto.

AMAZING MIGRATIONS

CONTENTS

Words that look like **this** can be found in the glossary on page 24.

The place where an animal lives is called its habitat. A good habitat has food, water and a safe place for an animal to raise their **young**.

Germany

Australia

Although these forests look similar, they experience different types of weather. This makes them very different habitats.

There are many types of habitat and each one is different.

HOW DO HABITATS HELP ANIMALS?

Animals live in habitats that meet their needs. Some habitats meet the needs of lots of different animals so there will be many **species** living there.

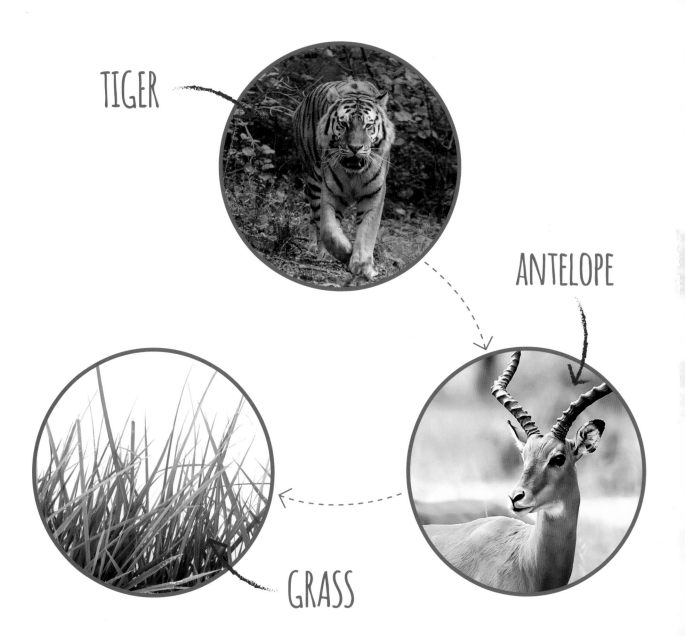

TIGER

ANTELOPE

GRASS

Some habitats might have plants that animals use for food or shelter. Some animals eat other animals in their habitat to survive. This is called a food chain.

WHAT DOES MIGRATION MEAN?

Migration is the movement of animals from one place to another. Some animals move small distances when they migrate. Others travel hundreds of kilometres.

Sometimes, thousands of animals migrate at the same time.

Animals that live on land often migrate in groups. They stay together for **protection** from other animals.

Animals often migrate to find better **living conditions**. During the winter months, some animals move to warmer places with more food.

Frogs migrate to shallow ponds so that they can mate.

Some animals migrate so that they can **mate**, give birth or lay eggs in a particular place.

THE GREAT MIGRATION

Wildebeest

The Great Migration happens once a year in Africa. This migration includes over one million wildebeest as well as other animals, such as zebras.

The animals migrate across the countries of Tanzania and Kenya. They migrate so that they can give birth to their young and find more food and water.

The Mara River, Kenya, during the Great Migration

THE CARIBOU

Caribou are a species of deer that live in North America. Caribou spend summer in **grasslands** and migrate south in winter to find more food.

Caribou

Up to 50,000 caribou will migrate at the same time.

A herd of caribou will travel thousands of kilometres when they migrate. They have one of the longest journeys of all migrating animals.

CHRISTMAS ISLAND CRABS

CHRISTMAS
ISLAND

AUSTRALIA

Christmas Island is an island near Australia.
It is home to tens of millions of red crabs.

Every year, during the wet season, the red crabs migrate from the forests to the coast. They do this so the females can lay eggs.

EARTHWORMS

Earthworms live in soil. Earthworms migrate **vertically**, burying downwards to move away from cold temperatures at the **surface** of the soil.

As the weather becomes warmer, the earthworms move back to the surface of the soil. This keeps them warm but makes it easier for birds to eat them.

The Earth is becoming hotter over time because of something known as climate change. Climate change is causing **weather patterns** to change.

Animals rely on the seasons changing to tell them when to migrate. If weather patterns change unexpectedly, animals can become confused and migrate at the wrong time.

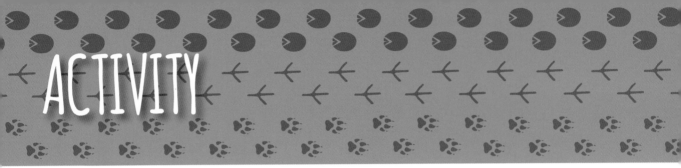
1. Draw a picture of the four different seasons. Think about all the changes you see and feel during each one. Do the trees have lots of leaves or none at all? Is the sun shining or is it raining?

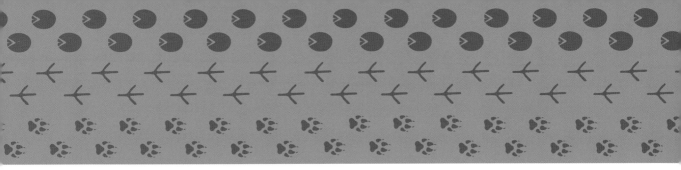

2. Add labels to your drawing to explain in more detail.

3. Which animals do you often see during each season? Do they disappear at different times of the year? Add the animals to each of your drawings!

GLOSSARY

grasslands	large areas of land covered with grass
living conditions	the things that affect the way something lives
mate	to produce young with an animal of the same species
protection	looking after or keeping safe
similar	being alike but not exactly the same
species	a group of very similar animals or plants that are able to produce young together
surface	the outer part of something
vertically	in an 'up' or 'down' direction.
weather patterns	weather that we have become used to happening at particular times
young	an animal's offspring

INDEX